KT PUBLISHING
CRAFTING TALES FOR EVERY TRAIL

UNICORN
COLORING SHEETS

With
Informative
Facts

INTRODUCTION

Welcome to the magical world of Unicorns

This Unicorn Coloring Book is specially designed just for you, to let your creativity run wild and make these mythical beings come to life with your own unique flair.

With each page you color, you'll step into a world of rainbows, sparkles, and dreams.

So grab your favorite coloring tools, put on your thinking cap, and let the journey begin. Whether you're a budding artist or simply love unicorns, there's no limit to the magic you can create.

So, let your inner artist shine and let the coloring fun begin!

UNICORN
COLORING SHEETS
FOR KIDS

THIS BOOK BELONGS TO

_____

_____

_____

TEST COLOR PAGE

Unicorns are mythical creatures often depicted as horse-like animals with a single horn on their forehead.

The word "unicorn" comes from two Latin words: "uni" meaning one, and "cornu" meaning horn.

Unicorns are known for their beauty, grace, and purity.

They are believed to be gentle and kind creatures.

Legends of unicorns have been around for centuries, dating back to ancient civilizations.

Unicorn horns are said to have magical powers, like healing and purifying water.

Some believe that unicorn sightings were actually encounters with rhinoceroses.

Unicorn stories are prevalent in many different cultures around the world.

Unicorns are often associated with rainbows and bright colors.

They are considered symbols of hope and positivity.

In Greek mythology, unicorns were said to be tamed by virgins.

Unicorn hair is sometimes used in the making of wands in the Harry Potter series.

Unicorns have appeared in numerous books, movies, and TV shows.

Scotland's national animal is the unicorn.

Unicorns are often depicted as white, but they can come in various colors.

Some unicorn myths describe them as being able to fly.

The unicorn is the official animal of the city of San Francisco, USA.

They are sometimes called "alicorns" when referring to their horns.

Chinese unicorn, known as "Qilin," is a blend of different animals and is considered a symbol of good luck.

Unicorns are often associated with the zodiac sign Pisces.

The unicorn is one of the symbols on the coat of arms of the United Kingdom.

Unicorn-themed merchandise, like toys and clothing, is very popular.

Some people believe that unicorns still exist in remote, unexplored areas of the world.

Unicorns are often featured in fairy tales and fantasy literature.

In some cultures, unicorn horns were thought to neutralize poisons.

Unicorn names are often whimsical and magical, like "Starshine" or "Twinkle."

Unicorns are sometimes associated with the moon.

Unicorns are sometimes portrayed as
protectors of the forest and its creatures.

The unicorn is a popular theme for baby nurseries and children's bedrooms.

The unicorn is mentioned in the Bible in several passages.

Some unicorn legends suggest that they can live for centuries.

The unicorn is often used as a symbol for imagination and creativity.

Unicorns are often associated with the element of water.

Unicorn symbolism is often used in advertising and branding.

In some stories, unicorns are shy and elusive, making them hard to find.

The unicorn is often used as a symbol for imagination and creativity.

Some believe that unicorns are guardians of hidden treasures.

Unicorns are often shown with flowing manes and tails.

Unicorns are sometimes depicted with wings,
making them even more magical.

In Scotland, unicorns are often associated with the monarchy.

Unicorns have been featured in art throughout history.

In some stories, only those with a pure heart can see a unicorn.

Unicorn-themed parties and decorations are popular for birthdays and celebrations.

In some cultures, unicorn horns were thought to neutralize poisons.

The unicorn is a popular symbol for LGBTQ+ pride.

Unicorns are creatures of wonder and enchantment, bringing magic into our lives.

CONGRATULATIONS, COLORING CHAMPION!

Wow! You've completed this Unicorn Coloring Book with flying colors! Your creativity has transformed each page into a magical masterpiece.

But guess what? Your coloring adventures are just beginning! Keep exploring, keep coloring, and keep making the world more colorful with your amazing talent.

You're a true artist, and we can't wait to see all the incredible art you'll create next. Keep spreading joy and magic wherever you go!